MY FIRST
MASS BOOK

Edited by Bart Tesoriero
Illustrations by Jepree Manalaysay

Nihil Obstat: Right Reverend Archimandrite Francis Vivona, S.T.M., J.C.L.
Imprimatur: Most Reverend Joseph A. Pepe, D.D., J.C.D.
Date: May 12, 2011

Published with the approval of the Committee on Divine Worship,
United States Conference of Catholic Bishops.

Library of Congress Control Number: 2011910783
ISBN 978-1-936020-24-9

INTRODUCTORY RITES

ENTRANCE SONG

Together we make the Sign of the Cross:

Priest: In the name of the Father, and of the Son,
and of the Holy Spirit.

People: Amen.

GREETING

The priest greets us in the name of the Lord:

A Priest: The grace of our Lord Jesus Christ,
and the love of God,
and the communion of the Holy Spirit
be with you all.

Or

B Priest: Grace to you and peace from God our Father
and the Lord Jesus Christ.

Or

C Priest: The Lord be with you.

We reply:

People: And with your spirit.

THE PENITENTIAL ACT

Priest: Brethren (brothers and sisters), let us acknowledge our sins,
and so prepare ourselves to celebrate the sacred mysteries.

Priest and People:
I confess to almighty God
and to you, my brothers and sisters,
that I have greatly sinned,
in my thoughts and in my words,
in what I have done and in what I have failed to do,

We strike our breast:
through my fault, through my fault,
through my most grievous fault;

We continue:
therefore I ask blessed Mary ever-Virgin,
all the Angels and Saints,
and you, my brothers and sisters,
to pray for me to the Lord our God.

Priest: May almighty God have mercy on us,
forgive us our sins, and bring us to everlasting life.
People: Amen.

THE KYRIE

Priest: Lord, have mercy.
People: Lord, have mercy.
Priest: Christ, have mercy.
People: Christ, have mercy.
Priest: Lord, have mercy.
People: Lord, have mercy.

THE GLORIA

Glory to God in the highest,
and on earth peace to people of good will.

We praise you,
we bless you,
we adore you,
we glorify you,
we give you thanks for your great glory,
Lord God, heavenly King,
O God, almighty Father.

Lord Jesus Christ, Only Begotten Son,
Lord God, Lamb of God, Son of the Father,
you take away the sins of the world,
    have mercy on us;
you take away the sins of the world,
    receive our prayer;
you are seated at the right hand of the Father,
    have mercy on us.

For you alone are the Holy One,
you alone are the Lord,
you alone are the Most High,
Jesus Christ,
with the Holy Spirit,
in the glory of God the Father. Amen.

THE COLLECT

We pray silently with the Priest, who then prays the Collect prayer.

People: Amen.

LITURGY OF THE WORD

SIT

THE FIRST READING

God Speaks to Us through the Old Testament

The lector proclaims God's Word
as spoken through His Prophets and Apostles.

At the end of the reading:
Lector: The word of the Lord.
People: Thanks be to God.

RESPONSORIAL PSALM

The cantor proclaims the psalm, and we respond.

THE SECOND READING

God speaks to us through the New Testament.

At the end of the reading:
Lector: The word of the Lord.
People: Thanks be to God.

STAND

GOSPEL ACCLAMATION

The cantor sings the Alleluia
and we repeat it.

During Lent, other acclamations are used.

THE GOSPEL
God gives us Good News!

Jesus proclaims His Gospel to us
through the Priest or Deacon.

Deacon (or Priest): The Lord be with you.
People: And with your spirit.

Deacon (or Priest): A reading from the holy Gospel according to N.

People: Glory to you, O Lord.

The Priest or Deacon proclaims
God's Word as we listen.

At the end of the Gospel:

Deacon (or Priest): The Gospel of the Lord.

People: Praise to you, Lord Jesus Christ.

SIT   THE HOMILY

In the Homily the Priest speaks about God's Word we have just heard in
the Readings. He helps us understand what God is saying to us and
encourages us to obey God and do what Jesus tells us.

THE PROFESSION OF FAITH

The Nicene Creed

I believe in one God,
the Father almighty,
maker of heaven and earth,
of all things visible and invisible.

I believe in one Lord Jesus Christ,
the Only Begotten Son of God,
born of the Father before all ages.
God from God, Light from Light,
true God from true God,
begotten, not made, consubstantial with the Father;
through him all things were made.
For us men and for our salvation
he came down from heaven,

(All bow during the next three lines.)

and by the Holy Spirit was incarnate
of the Virgin Mary,
and became man.

For our sake he was crucified under Pontius Pilate,
he suffered death and was buried,
and rose again on the third day
in accordance with the Scriptures.
He ascended into heaven
and is seated at the right hand of the Father.
He will come again in glory
to judge the living and the dead
and his kingdom will have no end.

I believe in the Holy Spirit, the Lord, the giver of life,
who proceeds from the Father and the Son,
who with the Father and the Son is adored and glorified,
who has spoken through the prophets.

I believe in one, holy, catholic and apostolic Church.
I confess one Baptism for the forgiveness of sins
and I look forward to the resurrection of the dead
and the life of the world to come. Amen.

The Apostles' Creed

The Apostles' Creed may be used especially during Lent and Easter Time.

I believe in God,
the Father almighty,
Creator of heaven and earth,
and in Jesus Christ, his only Son, our Lord,

(All bow during the next two lines.)

who was conceived by the Holy Spirit,
born of the Virgin Mary,
suffered under Pontius Pilate,
was crucified, died and was buried;
he descended into hell;
on the third day he rose again from the dead;
he ascended into heaven,
and is seated at the right hand of God the Father almighty;
from there he will come to judge the living and the dead.

I believe in the Holy Spirit,
the holy catholic Church,
the communion of saints,
the forgiveness of sins,
the resurrection of the body,
and life everlasting. Amen.

PRAYER OF THE FAITHFUL

People: Lord, hear our prayer.

The Priest ends with a prayer:

People: Amen.

LITURGY OF THE EUCHARIST

SIT **PRESENTATION AND PREPARATION OF THE GIFTS**
We offer gifts of bread and wine,
which will become the Body and Blood of Christ. We sing an Offertory
Song while the gifts are brought forward.

The Priest takes the host and prays quietly:

Blessed are you, Lord God of all creation,
for through your goodness we have received
the bread we offer you:
fruit of the earth and work of human hands,
it will become for us the bread of life.

If there is no Offertory Song, the Priest may
pray this prayer aloud, and we respond:

People: Blessed be God for ever.

The Priest pours wine and a little water into the chalice, praying quietly:

By the mystery of this water and wine
may we come to share in the divinity of Christ
who humbled himself to share in our humanity.

The Priest raises the chalice slightly, praying quietly:

Blessed are you, Lord God of all creation,
for through your goodness we have received
the wine we offer you:
fruit of the vine and work of human hands,
it will become our spiritual drink.

*If there is no Offertory Song, the Priest may pray this prayer aloud,
and we respond:*

People: Blessed be God for ever.

STAND   **INVITATION TO PRAYER**

Priest: Pray, brethren (brothers and sisters),
that my sacrifice and yours
may be acceptable to God,
the almighty Father.

**People: May the Lord accept the sacrifice at your hands
for the praise and glory of his name,
for our good
and the good of all his holy Church.**

PRAYER OVER THE OFFERINGS

We Pray that God Will Accept Our Gifts

The Priest prays over the offerings. We respond:
People: Amen.

EUCHARISTIC PRAYER II

The Priest invites us to join him in the Eucharistic Prayer.
The Preface Dialogue

Priest: The Lord be with you.

People: And with your spirit.

Priest: Lift up your hearts.

People: We lift them up to the Lord.

Priest: Let us give thanks to the Lord our God.

People: It is right and just.

The Preface

The Priest prays the Preface. Together with him we thank and praise God for who He is and for loving us in so many wonderful ways. We especially thank Him for the gift of His Son Jesus Christ, the Savior He sent to redeem us. We join the angels and saints in giving glory to God, as we say:

The Sanctus

Priest and People:
Holy, Holy, Holy Lord God of hosts.
Heaven and earth are full of your glory.
Hosanna in the highest.
Blessed is he who comes in the name of the Lord.
Hosanna in the highest.

KNEEL

You are indeed Holy, O Lord,
the fount of all holiness.
Make holy, therefore, these gifts, we pray,
by sending down your Spirit upon them like the dewfall,
so that they may become for us
the Body and ✤ Blood of our Lord Jesus Christ.

At the time he was betrayed
and entered willingly into his Passion,
he took bread and, giving thanks, broke it,
and gave it to his disciples, saying:

TAKE THIS, ALL OF YOU, AND EAT OF IT,
FOR THIS IS MY BODY,
WHICH WILL BE GIVEN UP FOR YOU.

The Priest raises the consecrated Host for all to see and worship.

In a similar way, when supper was ended,
he took the chalice
and, once more giving thanks,
he gave it to his disciples, saying:

TAKE THIS, ALL OF YOU, AND DRINK FROM IT,
FOR THIS IS THE CHALICE OF MY BLOOD,
THE BLOOD OF THE NEW AND ETERNAL COVENANT,
WHICH WILL BE POURED OUT FOR YOU AND FOR MANY
FOR THE FORGIVENESS OF SINS.

DO THIS IN MEMORY OF ME.

The Priest raises the Chalice so all can see and worship.

The Memorial Acclamation

Priest: The mystery of faith.

People: We proclaim your Death, O Lord,
and profess your Resurrection
until you come again.

Therefore, as we celebrate
the memorial of his Death and Resurrection,
we offer you, Lord,
the Bread of life and the Chalice of salvation,
giving thanks that you have held us worthy
to be in your presence and minister to you.
Humbly we pray
that, partaking of the Body and Blood of Christ,
we may be gathered into one by the Holy Spirit.
Remember, Lord, your Church,
spread throughout the world,
and bring her to the fullness of charity,
together with **N.** our Pope and **N.** our Bishop
and all the clergy.
Remember also our brothers and sisters
who have fallen asleep in the hope of the resurrection,
and all who have died in your mercy:
welcome them into the light of your face.
Have mercy on us all, we pray,
that with the Blessed Virgin Mary, Mother of God,
with the blessed Apostles
and with all the Saints who have pleased you throughout the ages,
we may merit to be coheirs to eternal life,
and may praise and glorify you
through your Son, Jesus Christ.

The Priest raises the Host and Chalice for all to see:

Priest: Through him, and with him, and in him,

O God, almighty Father,

in the unity of the Holy Spirit,

all glory and honor is yours,

for ever and ever.

People: Amen.

STAND   # COMMUNION RITE

THE LORD'S PRAYER

Priest and People: Our Father, who art in heaven,

hallowed be thy name;

thy kingdom come,

thy will be done on earth as it is in heaven.

Give us this day our daily bread,

and forgive us our trespasses,

as we forgive those who trespass against us;

and lead us not into temptation,

but deliver us from evil.

Priest: Deliver us, Lord, we pray, from every evil,

graciously grant peace in our days,

that, by the help of your mercy,

we may be always free from sin

and safe from all distress,

as we await the blessed hope

and the coming of our Savior, Jesus Christ.

People: For the kingdom, the power and the glory are yours,
now and for ever.

THE SIGN OF PEACE

With hands extended, the Priest prays for peace, ending with:

Priest: Who live and reign for ever and ever.

People: Amen.

Priest: The peace of the Lord be with you always.

People: And with your spirit.

Priest: Let us offer each other the sign of peace.

We give one another a sign of peace.

THE FRACTION OF THE BREAD

The priest breaks the bread, showing that
we are all members of the one Body of Christ.

We sing or say:

**Lamb of God, you take away the sins of the world,
have mercy on us.**

**Lamb of God, you take away the sins of the world,
have mercy on us.**

**Lamb of God, you take away the sins of the world,
grant us peace.**

KNEEL

We speak to Jesus in our heart:
"Dear Jesus, I love You!
Please come into my heart,
and fill me with Your love."

Lord Jesus Christ, Son of the living God,
who, by the will of the Father
and the work of the Holy Spirit,
through your Death gave life to the world,
free me by this, your most holy Body and Blood,
from all my sins and from every evil;
keep me always faithful to your commandments,
and never let me be parted from you.

Or

May the receiving of your Body and Blood,
Lord Jesus Christ,
not bring me to judgment and condemnation,
but through your loving mercy
be for me protection in mind and body,
and a healing remedy.

INVITATION TO COMMUNION

Priest: Behold the Lamb of God,
behold him who takes away the sins of the world.
Blessed are those called to the supper of the Lamb.

Priest and People:
Lord, I am not worthy
that you should enter under my roof,
but only say the word
and my soul shall be healed.

COMMUNION

The Priest receives the Body and Blood of Christ.

Priest: The Body of Christ.
Communicant: Amen.
Priest: The Blood of Christ.
Communicant: Amen.

The Communion Song
We sing the Communion Song together as we receive Communion.

Period of Silence or Song of Praise

PRAYER AFTER COMMUNION

Priest: Let us pray.

STAND   *The Priest prays the Prayer after Communion, ending with:*
Priest: Through Christ our Lord.
People: Amen.

CONCLUDING RITES

God has fed us with His Word and the Body of Christ.
Let us go now to do good works as we praise and bless the Lord.

THE FINAL BLESSING

Priest: The Lord be with you.
People: And with your spirit.
Priest: May almighty God bless you,
        the Father, and the Son, ✠ and the Holy Spirit.
People: Amen.

DISMISSAL

Deacon (or Priest):

A   Go forth, the Mass is ended.

B   Go and announce the Gospel of the Lord.

C   Go in peace, glorifying the Lord by your life.

D   Go in peace.

People: Thanks be to God.

PRAYER AFTER MASS

O Jesus, You have just come to me in Holy Communion.
Your Body is living in my body.
Your Heart is beating in my heart.
You are truly present in me now.

Thank You so much for coming into my heart!
I am so glad You are here with me.
Please don't ever leave me.
I love You, Jesus.
I want to live forever with You in heaven.

Today I give myself to You.
I give You my body, my mind, and my heart.
Please keep me close to Your Heart,
and bring me back to You if ever I stray from You.

Jesus, I love You. Amen.